the guide to owning a
Conure

David Boruchowitz

T.F.H. Publications, Inc.
One TFH Plaza
Third and Union Avenues
Neptune City, NJ 07753

This book has been published with the intent to provide accurate and authoritative information in regard to the subject matter within. While every precaution has been taken in preparation of this book, the publisher and author assume no responsibility for errors or omissions. Neither is any liability assumed for damages resulting from the use of the information herein.

Printed and bound in China
06 07 08 09 10 3 5 7 9 8 6 4

ISBN 0-7938-2016-2

www.tfhpublications.com

Contents

What is a Conure?

The name conure comes from an old genus name, *Conuris*, which signifies "cone-tail" and refers to the long, pointed tail of these psittacine birds, which is visualized as a portion of a very tapered cone. These birds straddle the line between parrot and parakeet, with the smallest being just larg-

With their intelligent and fun-loving nature, conures have won the hearts of countless companion bird owners.

Conures are a great choice for people who want a bird with the characteristics and features of a larger parrot—but not the cost.

er than a budgie and the largest almost matching size with the smallest macaws. Which genera should be included in the group is somewhat in dispute. This is because there is no taxonomic division that corresponds exactly to the name conure. The old lump-all genus *Conuris* has given way to several modern genera, and the taxonomy continues to be revised. For example, there is disagreement over whether the Quaker parakeet, *Myiopsitta monachus*, is a conure. Even the related and similar *Pionus* and *Brotogeris* parrots are included by some as "conures."

All birds that are considered conures are in the subfamily Aratinginae, which also includes all of the macaws. Besides the Quaker, this subfamily also contains the probably extinct *Ognorhynchus icterotis* (the yellow-tailed parrot or conure), and the long-extinct Carolina parakeet or conure, *Conuropsis carolinensis*. Because all other neotropical parrot species belong to some other subfamily of the family Aratingidae, we can for the purposes of this book define "conures" as neotropical parrots in the subfamily Aratinginae that are not macaws. Even this, of course, is an arbitrary decision and in itself raises the question of what is a macaw.

One might be tempted to suggest that macaws have a bare facial patch, while conures have at most a bare periophthalmic ring, but Hahn's macaw, *Diopsittaca nobilis*, is intermediate in this regard, and, of course, the large blue macaws of the genera *Anodorhyncus* and *Cyanopsitta* have conure-like eye rings instead of bare facial patches. The Nanday conure's (*Nandayus nanday*) eye ring is very prominent as well.

Thus, it is clear that the distinctions we make in our naming systems are only partially reflected in the birds themselves. In many ways a Patagonian conure (*Cyanoliseus patagonus*) seems much more like a macaw than it does like some conures (e.g., the genus *Pyrrhura*). As for other subfamilies, the other major one is Amazoninae, with the Amazons, Pionus, and similar parrots. Of the remaining, none are very prevalent in the pet trade. The canary-winged parrots (subfamily Brotogeryinae) and the caiques (subfamily Pionitinae) are gaining popularity and coming down in price as breeding programs are established and the birds' reputations are being made known. These birds are similar in many ways to the conures and share some of the same appeal. Their husbandry is also similar, so much of what we discuss in this book could apply to these species as well.

For the sake of this book we will include all those birds commonly called conures, plus the Quaker, or, in other words, all species in Aratinginae that are not known as macaws. Whatever you call them, conures are wonderful pet birds. They are intelligent, affectionate, and fun loving. Although most are not known as great talkers, many do learn several words, and a few do very well. This is a diverse group, and we will discuss the particulars about each group of species in a latter part of this book.

Conures are a common choice for someone who wants to "step up" from budgies and cockatiels, but who is not ready for the commitment required by a large macaw, Amazon, or cockatoo. They are about the size of a cockatiel (some are even smaller), but they have many of the features of larger parrots. In many ways they are miniature versions of the macaws, with their powerful beaks, large heads, bright colors, comical, acrobatic ways, and talents for mimicry.

Housing Your Conure

Before you can select a conure as a pet, you must have suitable accommodations for it. Many conures wind up spending most of their time free, interacting with their human "flock," but your bird will need a place to call home even if the door is always left open and it only goes in to eat and to sleep. And, of course, there will be times when your bird will have to be locked in its cage, even if it is only when you have your doors open for deliveries or repairs or when the bird has to be left alone in the house. It is almost never safe to leave a parrot unsupervised; there are too many ways it can injure or be injured by household objects.

Although your conure may prefer to spend time out of his cage with you, he will still need a cage to return to for refuge and rest.

CAGE

The type of cage you get depends on several things, the most important of which is whether you plan to keep your bird in its cage most of the time. Conures are active birds and need room to exercise. If they are let out regularly, they will get plenty of exercise flying around and playing with you, so their cage can be smaller—just big enough for them to flap their wings fully extended. If, on the other hand, your pet will spend much of its time in the cage, it must be big enough to allow unfettered flight from a perch at one end to a perch at the other. For the smaller Pyrrhura conures, this might be a 24-inch cage, but for birds the size of Blue Crowns, 48 inches would be a reasonable minimum length.

Conures, like almost all parrots, are climbers, pulling themselves along with their powerful beak. For this reason, a cage with all vertical bars is not as suitable as one that is made of rectangular mesh or horizontal wires. In such a cage, the bird will make use of all six inside surfaces—though of them all, the bottom is often the least used, since conures are climbers, not walkers. Conures of the genus Aratinga (Suns and Jendays) especially like the top of their cages for hanging upside down and numerous other acrobatic tricks.

Ideally, the cage will have a wire mesh floor over the dropping pan, which should be lined with newspaper that is changed daily.

Perches should be of various diameters. Natural branches from nonpoisonous trees are perfect. If you have access to wild grapevines, these make fantastic perches, and your conure will

In choosing a cage, consider your conure's penchant for climbing and hanging upside-down. This Queen of Bavaria conure is quite an acrobat.

have a ball shredding off the bark and then whittling away at the wood. Whether natural branches or dowels, the perches will need occasional replacing as they get chewed up. Your bird will use a perch as a perch, of course, but also as a jungle gym, beak sharpener, chew toy, and trapeze. Imaginative placement of the perches will provide maximum play area, while still allowing free flight.

Manufacturers offer several alternatives to the traditional wooden perch. There are plastic perches, which are easily cleaned, and also braided rope perches, which can be bent into a variety of configurations and that offer a softer foothold for your bird. Also available are concrete and lava rock perches. One of these in your conure's cage will help keep its toenails trimmed, and it will also help the bird keep its beak from overgrowing.

It's best to have a couple of sturdy food crocks, and either another one for water or a water bottle. Most birds quickly learn to use a water bottle, which is quite advantageous because the water stays much cleaner than it does in an open bowl. If you wish to use a bottle and your bird has not been trained to it, make sure that it is drinking from the bottle before you remove the water cup. Parrots are naturally curious, so if you tap at the tube, causing a couple of drops of water to drip out, your bird will probably come over to investigate. Many bird bottles have the ball valve colored red to attract the bird's attention. If you have more than one bird and one of them is trained to the bottle, the others will quickly imitate.

NESTS

Many conures prefer to sleep in a nest box, even when they are not breeding. It is reasonable to assume that depriving them of a nest box causes them distress or discomfort. They are perfectly capable of spending the night on a perch or clinging to the wire of the cage, but given a choice, they'll be snuggled up in a nest box.

The only real disadvantage to providing a sleeping nest box is that it

A trip to a local pet store will reveal a multitude of cage and accessory choices; keep in mind your space and budgetary restrictions, but purchase the largest cage you can.

Perches can be made of many materials—concrete, lava rock, and plastic—as well as natural branches and wooden dowels.

encourages pairs—and even single females—to breed, and breeding must be limited to prevent exhaustion of the birds and potentially fatal egg binding in the female. Conures are not so domesticated that they all breed nonstop, but there are pairs that do. (There are even pairs that will nest on the floor of the cage if there is no other provision.) So, what do you do if your bird keeps laying eggs and you don't want simply to remove the box?

One solution is the cloth nests or tents sold for just this purpose. These provide a cozy, snug spot for sleeping, but they generally do not meet a bird's requirements for a breeding nest site. You can also use open nest boxes, which instead of a front with an entrance hole, are simply open on the front. The bird can still go in and sleep partially enclosed, but it is not inclined to use such a place for egg laying.

TOYS

You will need toys for your conure. Being intelligent and social, these birds need something to do when you cannot play with them. Like a human toddler, a conure inspects any object it encounters—usually by chewing on it. Using one foot as a hand, the bird

Accessories such as perches, swings, and toys will help entertain your conure and encourage him to exercise.

Conures are fascinated by toys of all kinds, those found in pet stores as well as those that you yourself create.

will examine the item of interest, turning it this way and that, nibbling here and there. If there are projections or moving parts, they will be checked out—and often removed. It is important that any toys you give your bird are safe. With conures, this means toys made out of nontoxic materials, having no places the bird can get its neck stuck or get hung up on its leg band, and being either indestructible (unlikely) or of a type that will not produce dangerous pieces when the bird disassembles it.

Toys can be elaborate, and there are some on the market that are incredibly complex. Your bird will also enjoy something as simple as a chunk of two-by-four to whittle. It will, however, quickly become bored with any toy, so you need to switch them around. When it stops being interested in a toy, put it aside and replace it with a new one. Later, you can bring it back out, and your conure should greet it with renewed enthusiasm.

Parrots especially like to play with their food, and a toy that combines fun and eating will be a big hit with your pet. Such toys range from skewers onto which pieces of fresh fruit and vegetables can be placed to little cages into which you place a treat, and the bird has to pull it out piece by piece.

When you let your bird out to play, it will treat anything it encounters as a potential toy, including items it can damage or destroy, like your prize Boston fern, that antique end table, or a handmade quilt; this also includes items that can injure or kill the bird, such as live electric cords, your prize-but-poisonous Poinsettia plant, or a bottle of cleaning fluid.

PLAY STATIONS

The use of parrot gyms or play stations is an excellent compromise between keeping your bird caged and simply letting it have the run of the house. Some of these attach to the top of the bird's cage, and some are free standing. Typical features are ladders, swings, toys, food and water cups, a

Three-month-old Sun conures enjoy the fresh air and excitement of being outside. Clipped wings will prevent all birds, regardless of age, from flying away and possibly into trouble.

jungle gym, and ropes and chains for climbing. Although any bird will enjoy playing on these, a bird whose wings have been clipped will likely stay on one. True, it could flutter to the floor, but usually a clipped bird will not jump off. It is still unwise to leave a bird on a gym totally unsupervised, but if you are around to check on it occasionally, this can provide your conure with some out-of-cage time without your direct involvement.

TO CLIP OR NOT TO CLIP

The issue of clipping wing feathers to restrict a bird's flight is a complex and emotional one. The procedure, however, is extremely simple. With a pair

Observe someone with experience before attempting to do a wing clip. In general, only the outer flight feathers are cut back.

of sharp scissors, the flight feathers on one or both wings are cut back. This does not hurt the bird any more than it hurts to cut your hair, and at its next molt the cut feathers will be lost and normal ones will regrow.

Whether you wish to do this or not will depend on several factors. The up and down sides are that a clipped bird is much less likely to get lost, injured, or killed, but a fully flighted bird obviously delights in flying and will fly playfully around the house, looking for mischief from an aerial perspective. Many people trim the wings to tame and train their bird, then let them grow in with its next molt and let it remain flighted after that.

If you intend to take your bird outside your home, even in a carrier, it is a very good idea to clip its wings first. I could fill a book with heartbreaking stories of people who lost cherished and valuable birds in situations in which they were convinced the birds would not or could not fly off, but they did.

Yes, there are even a few people who keep pet birds at liberty, allowing them to fly into and out of their aviaries at will, but personally, I reserve that for homing pigeons and barnyard fowl, whose natural behavior includes a very strong return-to-roost component. Pet parrots are unsuited to flying free outside. They are not predator-savvy, they are not adapted to our often-urban environments, and their instincts when alarmed tell them to fly far and fast and to continue shrieking for the flock to follow. Unfortunately, that means that if your pet is startled while outside, you will probably never see it again. Don't tempt fate.

Nutrition and Feeding

Conures are good eaters. In the wild, they travel in flocks, feeding on leaves, shoots, fruits, nuts, berries, and seeds. In some areas they are serious pests, descending on grain fields and other farm crops. They are opportunistic feeders and will also eat insects, grubs, eggs, and small animals.

There is much controversy about the dietary requirements of all parrots, but, to be honest, there is about the dietary requirements of humans, too. Just consider the conflicting advice of 30, 20, and even 10 years ago regarding red meat, eggs, fats, etc. Fortunately, most people ignore the experts and simply eat a lot of different foods, so any deficiencies in one area are made up for by another. As far as we know, the nutritional needs of all parrots are not much different from your own. Food that is good for you is also good for your conure. Note that this does *not* mean that any food you eat is good for your conure, since it is also true that food that is not whole-

Good nutrition is critical to the health and long life of your conure.

some and healthful for you is not suitable for your pet. Caffeine, excess sugar or salt, grease, and alcohol should not be given to your conure, even if you choose to indulge. This is especially important to keep in mind if your bird likes to share your table.

BASIC DIET

So, what *should* you feed your bird? Plant material should make up the bulk of its diet. This can be a high-quality seed mix based on white millet and canary seed—a typical budgie mix—supplemented daily with fresh fruits and vegetables of all kinds. You can also provide some safflower and/or sunflower seed; these are higher in fat, so they should be fed sparingly. You do not, however, have to feed your conure

Make clean, fresh water—the kind that you would want to drink— available to your conure at all times.

any seed at all. Many bird owners recognize that an all-seed diet is terribly inadequate, and realize that birds often prefer seeds so strongly that they will eat nothing else if given the choice, so they feed a pelleted diet instead.

When people first began to realize deficiencies of a seed-only diet, some spoke of seeds as if they were poison, and they touted pellets as the only thing your bird should ever put in its mouth. Today reality has won out, and we know that either or both can form the foundation of a good diet, but that if for no other reason than variety, even "complete diet" pellets should be varied with supplemental foods.

It's advisable to make fresh fruits and vegetables a regular part of your conure's diet.

This Gold-Capped conure exhibits all of the signs of good health: clear eyes, proper weight, and good plumage.

To ensure the cleanliness of your bird's food, place perches beside rather than above the food dishes.

While a seed diet is deficient in many areas and requires extensive supplementation, proprietary pelleted diets are an excellent basic food and can be supplemented with fresh fruits and vegetables, and with treats. One of the favorite treats of any conure—of almost any hookbill for that matter—is raw peanuts in the shell. Just make sure they are unsalted. Even a tiny Green-Cheeked conure will deftly hold a peanut in its foot and expertly shell it to get to the goodies inside. Peanuts, like all legumes, are high in protein. They are also rather high in fat, so they should be treats, not dinner.

Another very good basic diet is a cooked bean-legume mixture. The exact ingredients don't matter, and they can be varied to provide a break in monotony for your bird. Simply mix together various uncooked peas, beans, and grains such as whole corn, wheat berries, and brown rice. Let soak overnight, then bring to a boil. Turn down the heat to keep it just boiling and cook until tender. For convenience, this can be frozen in single serving portions. Just take one out the night before and thaw it in the refrigerator for the next day's meal. When feeding this type of mixture, it is a good idea to offer it in the morning. After no more than a few hours, remove any uneaten food and discard it. Then, in the afternoon, you can feed seeds, pellets, or..."birdy bread."

There are hundreds of recipes for birdy breads being traded around. They are all basically cornbread with various birdy additions such as sunflower seeds, frozen mixed vegetables, whole eggs (shell and all, put through a blender), and sprouted seeds.

For the daily supplements, you can choose from dark green leafy vegetables, deep yellow vegetables, and fruits of all kinds—except avocados, which are reported to be toxic to parrots. Carrots, yams, broccoli, tomatoes, corn, peas, beans, oranges, grapes, melon (with seeds), spinach, parsley, peppers—anything that is available. These fresh, raw supplements provide enormous nutrition, especially vitamins and minerals. They can be varied with the season and are best fed in great variety. If you feed only strawberries for a while, you may find a bird that will then only eat strawberries. Parrots are creatures of habit, so it is important for them to learn the habit of accepting whatever is in the bowl as food. When they're never sure what that is going to be, they will be much less likely to attach significance to any particular foodstuff.

When food is fun, it is even more appealing. Sections of raw corn on the cob provide a snack, a toy, and a beak workout all in one. Stone fruits are treat-wrapped toys. A chunk of carrot is an easily handled food that is as much fun to whittle as a hunk of wood—and a lot tastier.

ANIMAL PROTEIN

Wild conures eat some animal material, mostly insects. They require a small amount of food derived from animals for essential amino acids and for certain vitamins. This can come from strips of lean, cooked poultry (it is perhaps a disturbing reality that birds eat birds). But there is an item in your kitchen that in itself contains every single nutrient necessary to grow an entire bird: an egg. Obviously, an egg has everything needed to make a bird, if you include the shell, since the calcium for the chick's bones comes from the shell.

I am a big proponent of feeding eggs to pet birds. They usually go crazy for them, and the nutrition is superb. Eggs are also easy and neat to feed. Simply hard boil an egg, cool it, and split it in half with a knife. Do not peel the shell

When all else fails in trying to encourage a conure to eat, spray millet can tempt even the most finicky bird.

New foods can be offered in the morning, when birds are hungry and more willing to try something different.

off the egg. Many pet birds are calcium deficient, and eggshells, which they really enjoy, are a perfect source of this important mineral. Most conures share an enthusiasm for this wholesome food. You should not feed eggs every day, for they are a rich food, but once a week or so will provide considerable nutritional benefit.

Some parrot owners feed their birds live mealworms. This is certainly not necessary, as it is with some softbills, and you can supply equivalent nutrition with eggs, meat, and dairy products. But many birds enjoy them. People who keep parrots in outside aviaries will tell you that it is a rare bug or worm that escapes the sharp eye of their birds, so if you wish to feed live food to your conure, it makes a good nutritional supplement. Again, such a menu

item should be considered a treat, not a basic foodstuff.

FINICKY FEEDERS

Conures rarely need to be coaxed to eat. If weaned to seeds, however, they can be difficult to acclimate to more complete diets. The keys to success in converting a seedeater are perseverance, persistence, and patience. There are many cases where a bird owner had to continue offering alternate foods on a daily basis for several years before a stubborn bird could finally be persuaded to try them.

A very effective way to convince such a bird to try something new is to let the bird watch you or another bird eating a food item. Not wanting to miss out, many will take that crucial first bite. I have gotten many birds to try new foods simply by placing their cages next to those of birds that will eat anything, and then feeding both the same foods. Of course, a bird can have real preferences, so if your conure refuses to eat a particular food, try an equivalent one—for example, carrots for sweet potatoes, spinach for parsley, birdy bread for bean mix, etc.

Hunger, of course, is a great motivator, so offer new foods first thing in the morning, and then give the usual food later. Mixing foods also sometimes gets their interest, but parrots are very good at sifting through their food dish and jettisoning anything they consider inedible.

Hygiene and Health

I use the word "hygiene" because it signifies both sanitation and health, and, indeed, the bulk of avian health problems can be avoided or eliminated with proper sanitation. We can break down hygiene concerns into four main areas.

Cleanliness is key to good health. People who own more than one bird know that two conures may make twice as much mess as one.

Many bird owners keep two sets of food and water dishes that are rotated between use and disinfecting and cleaning.

FEEDING

Birds are messy, and conures are no exception. Not only will they perch on or over a food or water bowl, they will fling food around their cage, bathe in their water bowl, getting their whole cage wet, and lift their food cups and dump them. All of which adds up to dirty feed, polluted water, and a wet and messy cage.

This mess can be minimized by using water bottles and spill-proof cups that bolt onto the side of the cage. When feeding fresh foods, it is best to have two sets of dishes. Every day you can use a fresh bowl, and remove the other to be cleaned and dried. Being exposed to the air, preferably upside down, for 24 hours, takes care of a lot of bacterial

growth problems. The same goes for water bottles. Use two and alternate, disinfecting one while the other is in use. These simple steps can eliminate a host of potential health problems.

CAGE CLEANING

There are a variety of methods of keeping a cage clean. The time-honored newspaper method is still one of the best. Having a wire mesh floor above the newspaper improves it even more, since conures love to shred newspaper and will quickly reduce their floor covering to confetti. Many natural litter materials are also available, but some of these have been implicated in serious impactions of the digestive tract. As difficult as birds can be to get them to try a new food, they are often all too willing

Although papers and other materials that line the bottom of a cage can be removed without disturbing your conure, you'll need to relocate your pet for regular, more thorough, cleaning.

Start your young conures off on the right foot; these four-week-old Green-Cheeked conures are clean, healthy, and happy.

to swallow things that they shouldn't. So for cost, convenience, and safety, newspaper is the material of choice.

You should change the paper daily. If there is a mesh floor that prevents the birds from reaching the paper and destroying it, you can place a thick pile of papers on the tray and remove the soiled top layer each day. This time-saver will not work if you are placing the paper directly on the cage bottom, since your pet will have no problem shredding a whole week's worth of newspapers at once.

Using paper has another major benefit—it enables you to monitor your bird's droppings. The droppings are composed of three portions: the dark portion, which is the bird's feces; the pasty white portion, which is urea, the substance birds use to eliminate nitrogenous wastes; and the clear, watery portion, which is the urine. The amount, nature, and consistency of the droppings can be affected by many things. If a change in the droppings cannot be explained by a change in the diet, it may be cause for concern. The newspaper then becomes an early warning device of possible health concerns.

BATHS

Most conures love to bathe. Although we think of bathing as a means of removing dirt from our bodies, birds do that quite effectively with preening, and, in fact, many birds do not bathe, or bathe only in dust. Other species use bathing as a means of conditioning and maintaining their feathers.

Bathing is especially important for the

This conure really gets into his bath. Be certain to provide bathing water in addition to drinking water.

many species of conures that come from tropical rainforest environments, since the humidity in our homes, especially during the winter, is much lower than what they naturally experience. In any case, conures usually take their baths very seriously and can become completely soaked. It only adds to their enjoyment when everything else in the room also gets soaked in the process.

For most birds, the more often the better when it comes to baths. When I have not given my parrots a bath in some time, they will contort themselves to dip various body parts into their water dishes to give me the hint.

For bathing, your bird needs a shallow pan or dish large enough for it to stand in comfortably. The bird will try to bathe in something as small as its water bowl, but it can only do a proper job when it can stand in the water and dip and fling it all over its body. Many also enjoy being misted with a sprayer and will raise their wings and turn to get evenly wet. Tame birds often like to get under faucets. In any case, for your bird, the bath ends not with a toweling, but with an extended preening session, getting every feather tucked properly in place and neatly arranged.

PREVENTIVE MAINTENANCE

As with a child, well visits are important for your conure's health. Yearly check-ups at the vet can provide a baseline record against which your veterinarian can judge your conure if it becomes ill, while the doctor keeps an eye on its overall health and on any changes that become apparent.

This, plus a proper diet and good hygiene practices, will in most cases keep your conure in perfect health. In the event of problems, an experienced avian veterinarian, rather than a book with some home diagnoses and remedies, is your best ally.

Taming, Training, and Talking

Many pet conures live in aviaries as part of a breeding program. They may or may not be hand-raised, and they may or may not talk. I myself have several breeding pairs of conures in which one is tame and will step right on my finger to get petted, while the other is not tame and will never do this. I also have a couple of pairs in which one of them talks and the other doesn't.

In such a setting, conures behave much as they do in the wild, interacting with other birds, vocalizing in raucous dawn and dusk "choruses." The tame ones will also interact with human beings when they are around, but all of the birds get along fine just in each other's company. There is nothing wrong with this situation, and some people prefer this to a tame, talking, trick-performing bird.

If, however, you wish to have a conure that is a friend as well as a pet, more a family member than a captive animal, it is useful to take a few moments to look at what it is about conures that makes them so easily assimilated into a human household,

Conures can make wonderful and affectionate companions, regardless of the level of training you wish to pursue.

Conures are among the many animal species that have traits that inspire people to collect, nurture, doctor, and propagate them.

and what that implies for the most effective way of teaching the bird.

Conures (and parrots in general) have many preadaptations that make them superior pets. Preadaptations, in biological terms, are traits that a species has that either are latent and become apparent or that change in application when there is a sudden change in the environment. Among conures' preadaptations for domestication are socialization, vocal communication, intense pair bonding, flocking behavior, high intelligence, bright colors, and problem-solving ability.

DOMESTICATION

It can be argued that the most successful species on earth are those that have traits that cause *Homo sapiens* to collect, nurture, doctor, and propagate them. Every plant or animal that is valuable to the human community lives a life of ease compared to their wild cousins, and they are often found at much higher population levels.

One of the traits most likely to get an animal domesticated is, for want of a better term, domesticatability—a combination of physical features and behavioral tractability. This tautological definition indicates that we do not know exactly what makes a species domesticatable.

Only a few animals are easily domesticated, and sometimes very closely

Taming your bird to step up onto your finger (or a stick) is the first step in more advanced training.

Young conures, such as these 13-week-old Green-Cheeks, are typically easier to train than older birds.

related species differ greatly in this regard. For example, the common ass or donkey, *Equus asinus*, was the first equid domesticated, many thousands of years ago, but the very similar onager or wild ass, *Equus hemionus*, is a nasty beast that has never been successfully domesticated. Likewise, the domesticated horse (*Equus caballus*) has a history almost as old as civilization, but the various zebras (*Equus* spp.) are barely trainable at best.

It is important to note that this is not simply a matter of getting an animal at or close to birth and raising it among humans. Raccoons, for example, make cuddly and irresistible pets when bottle-fed, but they become unpredictable and willful as adults and rarely remain suitable for household life. They lack whatever it is that makes a species amenable to domestic living. Dogs have it; wolves do not. Indian elephants have it; African elephants do not.

In a sense, pets or companion animals are the most domesticated of domesticated animals. These species are kept primarily as friends, even as family members by their human owners, and it is their "personalities" and appearance that are valued. The ubiquitous cat and dog come immediately to mind, and these animals have undergone such a long and steady domestication that there really are no wild counterparts to them. Biologists do not all agree on the original species. The same is true for one bird species—the society finch, found only in captivity, and whose hybrid origins are disputed. Most pet birds, however,

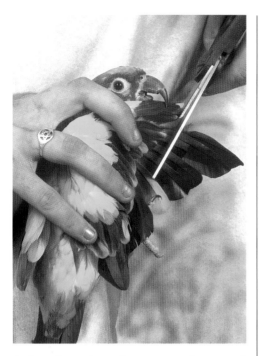

Indoor hazards such as open doors and windows abound, so wing clipping is advised for all birds, even those bird that won't be taken outside.

are relative newcomers to domestication, and in the case of many parrots, some pet specimens are even wild-caught animals.

INSTANT DOMESTICATION

This suggests that there is something different about parrots. Even after many generations of captive breeding, the ancient Romans found onagers extremely unpleasant under harness and always had to be on the alert for painful bites from these beasts of burden. Yet many parrots, conures included, have been trapped in the wild, brought into a loving home, and tamed, trained, and taught to speak.

Apes, dolphins, and parrots have in common that they are highly social

Although conures are not noted for excellent speaking skills, consistent training and interacting may encourage even the most stubborn ones to talk.

creatures with complex communication systems (gestural and facial for the apes, vocal for dolphins and parrots), and they are extremely intelligent. They also have an awareness of self, which means they enter into one-on-one relationships with other beings. All of these traits, of course, also apply to us humans. It is reasonable to assume that what makes these creatures so eminently domesticatable is that they actually domesticate themselves when placed in contact with friendly, supportive, and nurturing human beings.

A CONURE IN THE HOUSE

When a young conure is brought to a loving human home (and I highly

Food treats such as peanuts are an excellent incentive for conures in training.

Practice makes perfect when it comes to training. If your conure seems hesitant about stepping onto your hand, take a break and try again later.

recommend getting a young bird—just weaned if possible), it is at a stage in its social development that corresponds in the wild to leaving the nest and joining the flock. For a couple of months it has seen only its parents and the inside of a tree trunk, and after a short period of parental care and feeding in the outside world, it is expected to make it on its own. It is naturally programmed to be on the lookout, to be imitative, to be sociable. The example of the extended family of the flock provides a competent tutelage in finding food, avoiding predators, and doing all sorts of conure-ish things.

Many conures like to lie on their back in their owner's hand—a trick known as "playing dead."

To such a young conure, you, your family, and your home are its flock and forest. It looks to you to teach it, and it learns mostly by imitation. Keep this in mind when dealing with unwanted loud vocalizations—yelling at a screaming conure might make you feel better, but it will only escalate the cacophony.

Discipline

Your conure will want to please you and earn your praise. The most effective punishment you can administer is to convey your disappointment. If you scold or hit the bird, it will quickly become sullen and turn into a biter. If, on the other hand, you lavish it with praise when it behaves and turn a cold shoulder to it when it does not, the bird will quickly learn what is required to remain in your good graces.

Remember that your conure is an intelligent, inquisitive, fun-loving animal. It has a natural desire to do socially acceptable things and to please you. While many "experts" will disagree, any conure owner will tell you that the bond that develops between a bird and its human cannot be accurately described by any term other than *love*. In the same way that a dog that is loved and cherished becomes a loyal, loving companion, a conure treated the same way will respond in kind as well.

HOW DO I GET HIM TO TALK?

All parrots can be taught to "talk." Lovebirds can manage a squeaky

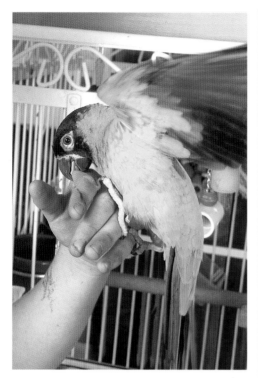

Like other parrots, conures will use their beak as a third "foot" while climbing or stepping onto a trainer's hand.

greater than interspecific differences. A particular conure might be a better talker than a particular Amazon. Overall, conures are not known for their great talking abilities; on the other hand, they are known as often making good talkers. The more you work with your bird, the better your chances are. Conures vocalize naturally, and many are excellent mimics. This would suggest that the way to teach a conure to talk is to talk to it.

The first thing you must do is provide the bird with motivation to speak. The most important factor here is isolation. If you have any other bird(s) around, your conure will probably prefer screeching and squawking with them to conversing with you. Even when the bird doesn't really understand the meaning of what it says,

word or two, or a short whistled tune. The large parrots—Amazons and Greys, for example—can learn dozens of words and even learn to string them together in meaningful sentences. Conures fall in between in ability, and much of the success in training a conure to speak depends on the dedication of the trainer.

While the speech of a conure is not going to have the clarity and diversity of the repertoire of an Amazon or an African Grey, most can master a few words, and the occasional conure will produce very clear speech. It is important, however, to remember that with parrots, as with any intelligent species, individual differences are often

Although conures are very vocal by nature, it will take patience and persistence to turn those squawks and screeches into words.

A young conure will look to his flock for guidance in learning behaviors and skills. As his owner, you are the conure's "flock leader" and responsible for this tutelage and socialization.

when it simply mimics your sounds, it does so out of a desire to communicate with you. If you were to observe a flock of conures feeding and playing, you would notice a constant, vocal back-and-forth, with excited bursts of noise for scary intruders, something new and interesting, or a tasty food source.

Likewise, when someone walks into a breeder's bird room with a pan full of fruits and veggies, the din is considerable. If you associate every feeding with the same repeated word, your conure will get the idea that your funny sequence of noises is your feeble attempt at the "here's the grub!" screech. Eventually, the bird may also use your funny noises to greet the food bowl.

Conures can be quite adventurous and prone to silly behavior. Here, a rambunctious pair explores the world of hanging indoor plants.

THE GUIDE TO OWNING A CONURE

Conures are clowns, and they enjoy being the center of attention. A Red-Masked conure strikes a pose and waits for applause.

Why do so many conures and other parrots say, "Pretty bird!"? Because so many people cuddle their parrots, scratching them and giving them attention and repeating over and over, "Pretty bird!" The birds learn to associate that sequence of sounds with cuddling and attention, and they probably hope that by imitating it, they will elicit the same.

Very often, a good talker will be speaking a word or two by the time it is weaned, so a baby that says "hello" or "up" is likely to add to its vocabulary. It is also the case that once a bird gets the idea of imitating human speech, it often learns new words more quickly. Remember, though, that there is enormous individual variation in a conure's ability/willingness to talk. If talking ability is extremely important, a Quaker or one of the larger parrots is your best bet. If, however, other conures appeal to you for other reasons, you may be pleasantly surprised by your pet's success with human speech.

TRICKS?

The natural playfulness, acrobatic talents, and curiosity of conures make it easy to teach them to do tricks. If a performing bird appeals to you, just remember two key words: repetition and reward. You may have seen a trained parrot perform a trick such as taking an envelope from its trainer, flying to a mailbox across the room,

Training is a great way to spend quality time with your conure, building a trusting relationship and having fun.

opening the box, placing the envelope in the box, closing it, raising the flag, and flying back to its owner for a treat. You can be sure that the training for that began with letting the bird grab the envelope (something it would be inclined to do in the first place) and rewarding it with praise and a tasty treat. After a while, the praise and treat were withheld until the bird took

the envelope and flew with it; then until the bird flew to the mailbox with the envelope; then until it also opened the box; etc.

There is no doubt, however, that parrots performing tricks are doing something more cerebral than a rat running a maze. They clearly understand *concepts* and do not need all parameters of a trick to remain constant, as long as they can grasp what the underlying concept is. I've watched macaws that were trained to fly to a volunteer standing in the audience, land on their outstretched arms, and retrieve dollar bills offered to them, which they took back to their trainers. The parrots had no way of knowing who the person would be, or where they would be standing, but they understood that *some* person would be standing *somewhere* in the audience.

It also seems evident to me that part of the reward for these performing birds is the applause of the audience. Most parrots are natural hams, and even if they're just wandering around your house, looking for mischief, they will keep looking over their shoulders at you, making eye contact, and checking out whether you are interested in and approving of what they're up to.

Types of Conures

This group of parrots has undergone a great deal of taxonomic revision recently. Most of this revision results from a splitting apart of the lump-all genus *Aratinga*, which once held about 20 species but is now reserved just for the Sun conure. The enormous variety of parrots once grouped

With the many types of conures now available, there is at least one to suit every person's needs and personality.

together have been identified into smaller genera, a couple of them being monotypic (having only one species).

Later chapters will detail the most commonly available species. In this one I will sketch in the taxonomy of the group. There are many species of conures, and before looking at them individually, it is helpful to gain an understanding of the subdivisions within the group. We can somewhat arbitrarily talk about three types of conures, and there are representatives from all three in the pet trade.

THE ARATINGA-TYPE

When you start looking at all the species of conures, it is easy to see why this batch was originally put

The Sun conure is an *Aratinga*-type conure, and perhaps the most recognized conure of all.

The Jenday conure is a colorful member of the *Aratinga*-type conures, a category of usual conure types.

together, not so much because of similarities they all have, but because of the fact that they are clearly not either of the other two types. These are the "usual" conures, the default category.

The group is diverse enough that I'll reserve descriptions of the individual species for a later chapter. For now, I'll just brief you on which birds we're talking about here.

Aratinga

The original *Aratinga* genus has become five. The four Sun-type conures, the Sun, Jenday, Gold-Fronted, and Gold-Capped, which were formerly separate species, have been collapsed as subspecies under *A. solstitialis*, the only species left in this genus.

Nandays

The common and inexpensive Nanday conure, *Nandayus nenday*, is in a genus of its own. It is close to the Sun conure in many ways, and its personality is much like the Sun's.

Psittacara

The genus *Psittacara* contains these seven species: *P. chloroptera, P. erythrogenys, P. euops, P. holochlora, P. leucophthalmus, P. mitrata,* and *P. wagleri*. These are the Christmas-colored conures—all over green with red highlights, often on the head. They are large birds, 12 to 15 inches long. There is variation in this group between species, subspecies, and individuals, and many captive animals are misidentified. The presence of hybrids only

The Blue-Crown conure is also known as the Sharp-Tailed conure.

complicates matters. All of these are intelligent, affectionate, and demanding pets, and many of them are very good talkers.

Thectocercus

Only one species wound up in this genus, *T. acuticaudata*. Various subspecies exist, known usually as Blue-Crowned or Sharp-Tailed conures. This is another large, intelligent conure with a large periophthalmic patch, all traits that emphasize the bird's closeness to the macaws.

Guaruba

The Golden or Queen of Bavaria conure from Brazil, *Guaruba guarouba,* is a special species. It is very threatened in the wild and rare in captivity, and you need a federal permit to keep

The Nanday conure shares many personality traits with the Suns.

The Mitred conure is one of seven green and red conures in the *Psittacara* genus. The conures in this genus can grow up to between 12 and 15 inches long.

and raise this bird. Its yellow coloration with green wings shows an affiliation to the Sun conure, but it is quite different and presents a unique appearance among the conures.

Eupsittula

There are 6 species in this genus: *E. astec (nana)*, *E. aurea*, *E. cactorum*, *E. canicularis*, *E. pertinax*, and *E. weddellii*. These are all small birds, about 10 to 12 inches long.

This genus contains the Brown-Throated conures, which are a taxonomic mess unto themselves. There are over a dozen recognized subspecies of *E. pertinax*, each with one or more sometimes overlapping common names. There is also dispute over whether *E. cactorum* is a separate species or actually *E. pertinax cactorum*—yet another subspecies of *E. pertinax*. Much of the problem here is due to the natural range of these birds, which includes several Caribbean

The Brown-Throated conure is one of six species in the *Eupsittula* genus, growing about 10 to 12 inches long.

THE GUIDE TO OWNING A CONURE

The Maroon-Bellied conure is a small bird that grows only eight or ten inches long.

islands, each with its own (or a couple of its own) subspecies. These all freely interbreed in captivity, and even sometimes in the wild, meaning that there are many subspecies hybrids around as well.

All are a basically green bird, with brownish throat and breast. One of the major variations is in the facial coloration, with some races having a completely yellow face all the way to those that show only a few yellow feathers.

Pyrrhura

The conures in this genus appear most similar to the brown throats. The overall coloration is green with a dark head, and common traits are a brown throat, maroon on the abdomen, and a neck ring or collar. These are also small birds, 8 to 10 inches long. There are 16 recognized species with many sub-

species variations, but you are likely to see only the Maroon-Bellied and the Green-Cheeked, *P. frontalis* and *P. molinae*. The typically small native ranges of the birds in this genus are sprinkled throughout southern Central and northern South America.

Oddments

There remain several conures that don't fit into either the *Aratinga* group or the *Pyrrhura*. Except for the Quaker, most of these birds are rather uncommon in aviculture.

Quakers

An extremely popular parrot, *Myiopsitta monachus* is a bit of an oddball as well as a leftover. The only parrot that builds a nest, it does so communally, with all of the pairs contributing to the huge nest of twigs. It is also unusual in its distinctive green and gray coloration.

The Green-Cheeked conure shares its small size and green coloring with the Maroon-Bellied.

Slender-Billed conures use their long beaks to dig for roots and shoots.

Southerners

The Slender-Billed conures (*Enicognathus* spp.) are the southernmost psittacine species in the world. They use their distinctive, oversized, slender upper mandible for digging in the ground, where they find roots and shoots to eat. Although they do not bear any particular resemblance to Quaker parrots, behaviorally there is an interesting similarity. Sometimes these parrots will build a nest of twigs within a crevice or hollow, often communally, and there is an account of one that built a freestanding nest of twigs in a tree.

The Patagonian Conure

Alone in its genus, *Cyanoliseus patagonus* is a large bird—18 inches—and it is attractively colored, overall olive, with lighter underparts, brown head, and orange under the abdomen. An affinity to the macaws is readily apparent.

Extinct?

Although some sources estimate as many as 200 individuals surviving, others report that *Ognorhynchus icterotis* is already extinct. It is not found in captivity.

Leptosittaca branickii

Another very rare species, the Golden Plumed conure is not found in captivity. Ironically, while it would undoubtedly be prized in an aviculturalist's collection, it is hunted in its native Colombia as an agricultural pest.

Rhynchopsitta pachyrhyncha

The Thick-Billed conure really looks very much like a macaw, especially in its named feature—its massive bill. This bird's range once included parts of the southwestern United States, but it is now confined to Mexico—a second U.S. parrot gone. Second? What's the first?

Gone Forever

The only parrot endemic to the United States, *Conuropsis carolinensis* has been extinct since the early part of this century. Despite its specific name, a subspecies was native as far north and inland as Wisconsin and Nebraska. I have not seen any detailed taxonomic studies of this species (or of its remains in museums), but on appearance alone, I would say that it is so reminiscent of a Sun or Jenday that there may have been a close affinity with *Aratinga*.

Breeding Your Conure

Conures are easily bred in captivity, and they are typically prolific, which is why they are so plentiful and so reasonably priced compared to, say, macaws or cockatoos.

SEXING

Obviously, to breed conures you must start with a male and a female. Since, however, conures are not sexually dimorphic, you cannot simply pick out one of each sex. There are two methods of accurately determining a bird's sex: surgical sexing (s/s) and blood testing (DNA).

Surgical sexing is a relatively simple procedure performed under anesthesia by a trained veterinarian and requires only laproscopic examination (a fiber optic device is threaded through a tiny incision). The sexual apparatus of the bird can be seen, and at the same time the doctor can check on its reproductive health. Typically, the bird is also given a thorough physical examination and tatooed with an identification number at the same time.

Breeding conures is a serious and time-consuming commitment, but the rewards are plentiful and enjoyable.

The idea in breeding conures in captivity is to duplicate as closely as possible the conditions that exist for them in the wild.

With blood testing, a drop of blood (from a pin prick or a pulled feather), is taken and sent to an avian testing laboratory. The chromosomes of the bird are examined, and the sex is evident. Both methods have their proponents, but DNA testing is gaining in popularity because of its simplicity—the breeder can prepare the sample and mail it off to the laboratory.

Once you have a known male and female, it does not necessarily mean that you have a breeding pair—they must be compatible. Fortunately, conures are not as particular as some of the larger parrots, but it is definitely not the case that any male and any female will get along. They form very strong pair bonds and are choosy about their mates. The safest bet is to buy a proven pair (meaning they have produced young together before) or a bonded pair (meaning that they have paired off, begun feeding each other, perhaps copulating and investigating nestboxes). There are, unfortunately, cases of someone paying for a proven or bonded pair and winding up with incompatible birds, or, even worse, two of the same sex, but most breeders are reputable and will give you accurate breeding records for the pair. As with any valuable purchase, get any guarantees in writing.

HYBRIDS

In the world of biology, textbook definitions often fall on their faces outside of the classroom. You probably know the definition of "species" as a group of organisms that can breed together and produce fertile offspring. Two classes of vertebrates, however, give this definition a lot of grief, especially when you consider captive animals. One class is Osteichthyes (bony fishes), and the other is Aves (birds). Fish and birds often freely interbreed—even individuals of different *genera*, and still produce fertile offspring. While this rarely happens naturally, it is so commonplace in captivity that for certain fish and birds it is almost impossible to find pure breeding stock.

Does it matter? Many will say no. Obviously, if the offspring are fertile and their offspring are fertile, there is nothing biologically *wrong* with these animals. It can be argued, however, that there is something wrong with the practice of mixing all of these genera and species. Each species of living things is a unique product of evolution. The same mindset that laments the loss of a species through extinction protests the wanton mixing of

Three-week-old conures requires round-the-clock attention and care, but will form strong bonds with their human "parents."

Pairs such as these Mitred conures may exhibit signs of breeding potential that include pairing off, feeding off each other, and next box investigating.

genetic lineages because it leads to the loss of the original, unique species. The animals themselves may or may not be compromised, but the world is a poorer place for the loss.

From the pet point of view, you might argue that a "Catalina" macaw (a hybrid of the Blue and Gold, *Ara ararauna*, and the Scarlet, *Ara macao*) is a wonderful companion bird—a beautiful addition to this earth, a human-made improvement like a cut and polished diamond. The problem is that no matter how many raw diamonds are cut and polished, the next raw diamond is unaffected. The Catalina macaw is neither a Blue and Gold nor a Scarlet, and it is fertile, so that it can breed with other macaws or with another Catalina, producing even more mixes, until you get something that is mistaken for a purebred macaw of one species, but that is not.

It is a difficult question. If we could be sure that a bird and all of its possible descendants will be unequivocally identified as hybrids forever, then, obviously, there is no real loss, and there may be considerable aesthetic gain. This, however, is not possible. The matter is further complicated with the issue of subspecies.

Subspecies are geographical variants of a single species and can easily and freely interbreed, and the question is made even more complicated by the uncertain taxonomy of parrots. Technically, a hybrid is an organism produced by two individuals of differ-

ent species. You must specify further if you use the term for matings of individuals from different subspecies of the same species—a hybrid of two subspecies. The Sun conure and the Jenday conure are significantly dissimilar in appearance. The Sun conure looks like it walked under several ladders where people were sloppily painting with different bright colors, and the Jenday conure looks like a bird those same people much more carefully painted in a precise pattern with those same bright colors. Is it okay to cross these two?

The "Sunday" conure (Sun x Jenday) is...well, under older taxonomies the Sun was *Aratinga solstitialis* and the Jenday was *Aratinga jendaya*. Now,

Although not apparent when first hatched, baby Sun conures will eventually develop striking bold yellow, red, and green coloration.

Some breeders prefer to remove young conure chicks from their parents, while others leave them and just pull them for feeding.

however, they are classified as *A. solstitialis solstitialis* and *A. solstitialis jendaya*. Obviously, it is not the case that older Sundays are hybrids while younger ones are merely subspecies crosses. But wait; it gets even more complicated.

Birds now classified in the genera *Thectocercus, Eupsittula, Psittacara,* and *Guaruba* used to be all listed in the genus *Aratinga*. So, what used to be considered a cross between two species is now defined as a cross between two genera.

I'll leave the detailed philosophical and ethical arguments for another forum. As a general rule, you should strive to match birds for breeding that are of the same species, and preferably of the same subspecies. If birds are the product of a hybrid mating, they should be identified as such to any potential purchasers.

BREEDING CAGES

Generally speaking, the bigger the better when it comes to breeding cages. Exercise is important for breeding birds; it not only maintains good health and vigor, it also improves fertility. A cage in which the birds can freely fly is required, and 6-, 7-, and 8-foot long flights are wonderful, even if smaller ones may be adequate.

Handfeeding is an extremely difficult process that should never be attempted by novices.

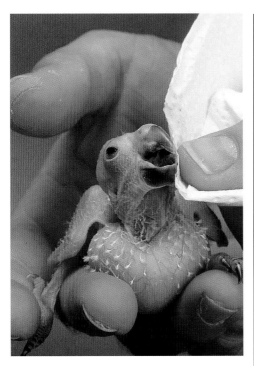

Cleanliness is critical in the early weeks of life. Wipe down young birds after they have been fed to prevent food from caking.

The other side of the coin, however, is that once they start breeding, the birds don't get much exercise. The female is going to spend months in the nest box, with only brief trips out, and the male will spend a lot of his time in or just outside the box. Many breeders take advantage of this fact and keep their breeders in very large, communal aviaries outside the breeding season. They then use smaller individual cages for breeding. This way the birds get their needed exercise, but breeding cages can be much more compact.

BREEDING SEASON

As is typical with semi-domesticated species like conures, some of the birds adhere to a natural breeding schedule, while others will breed any time of the year. Also, some birds will raise two or three clutches and then stop, while other pairs will keep on breeding until you remove the nest box. You should not permit more than three clutches per year to protect the health of the parents, though this may be a problem with birds that sleep in the box throughout the year.

NESTING

The nest box for a conure pair needs to be sized for the birds, but keep in mind that not all birds of the same species have the same preferences. Some pairs like it very cramped, while others want a little more room to spread out. Some males feed their

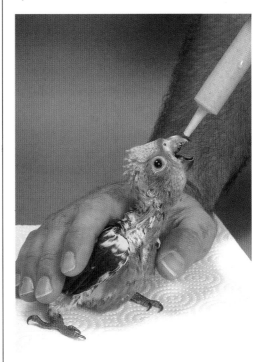

Although parent-raised conures are generally better breeders, handfed conures are in greater demand as pets.

mates through the opening, while others spend most of the time in the box. Often, if a pair seems ready to breed but does not produce eggs, a change in the size, shape, or position of the nest box will bring results.

In the wild, conures will nest in natural cavities, nest holes made by other animals, and in nests they themselves carve out. Quite a few species like to use burrows or crevices in steep, inaccessible cliffs. They usually "redecorate" to suit themselves no matter what the original nest was like. It is often a good idea to fill the nest box with some material—wood chips, sawdust, or cork, which the birds can remove to the extent and depth that they wish. This may decrease the

Chicks develop rapidly; by six weeks young conures begin to resemble their colorful parents.

If closed (permanent) bands are going to be used for identifying birds, be sure to attach them before the bird's foot has grown too large.

gnawing and destruction of the nest box itself, and it can also sometimes be especially useful with a pair that produces infertile clutches—because it takes time for them to set up house. When a female goes to nest too quickly, there may not have been enough time for the eggs to be fertilized, since an egg has to be fertilized before the white and shell are deposited on the yolk. Any eggs produced quicker than this after insemination will not be fertile. So, by delaying egg-laying, fertility can sometimes be increased.

Most conures will use a cockatiel nest box. The largest (e.g., Blue Fronts) may need a more spacious box, and the smallest ones (e.g., Green Cheeks) may use an English budgie size. Almost all conure pairs, if given a choice, will choose the small-

If hand-raised, a trio of Green-Cheekeds is likely to become very attached to its owners and will want to spend much of their time together.

est nest box into which they can squeeze. The most common method is to attach the box to the outside of the cage, with access through a hole cut in the wire mesh exactly opposite the next box opening. This cuts down on the destructive gnawing on the outside of the box, and it is easier to service the nest box, check on the birds and eggs, band the babies, etc. If the box is exterior, you must be certain that it is securely closed, and that you keep an eye on any escape holes the birds may gnaw into it.

FEEDING

Since the mother contributes nothing other than heat and moisture to the chicks between the laying of the eggs and hatching, obviously the hen's diet *prior* to egg-laying is crucial to the health of the hatchlings. She must have a high-protein, high-calcium, and vitamin-rich diet. While incubating, the parents should have the same diet to maintain them in optimum shape. Feeding a nest full of chicks is very demanding. And, of course, once the babies arrive, they will be fed whatever the parents eat, since they regurgitate food for their young. Adding extra soft foods like eggs, birdy bread, and fresh veggies and fruits makes the parents' job that much easier, and it provides a healthier diet for the babies.

THE GUIDE TO OWNING A CONURE

There are three ways to raise baby birds, and each method produces birds with desirable characteristics.

PARENT-RAISED

Parent-raised birds are usually called breeders, though many handfed birds are put into breeding programs, and some parent-raised birds are kept as caged pets. Parrots of all kinds, including conures, are such social and affectionate creatures that even wild-trapped birds are often tamed and become good friends with humans. Nevertheless, parent-raised birds are generally much less tame (and less expensive) than their hand-raised counterparts. Many aviculturalists find that parent-raised birds make the best breeders because all of their instincts seem well-developed. Certainly there is a lot of individual variation in parenting skills among conures of all types, however they were raised. Obviously, the only thing you need to do to produce parent-raised birds is to keep the parents well cared-for. These babies will not be able to be picked up, and they usually bite—hard—if you try. They can be tamed, but they are not naturally tame.

HANDFED

Handfed conures are in great demand. Taken from the nest soon after hatching (some breeders actually take the eggs and incubate them artificially, while others advocate letting the parents feed for a few weeks and then pulling the babies for handfeeding), these birds think they are people. They want to spend all of their time with humans, they give kisses, they preen your hair, they take showers with you, they eat what you eat, and they rarely bite unless provoked. They are curious, fearless, and spoiled. They also are usually the best talkers, since they want to be part of the human "flock" and gladly imitate people.

Handfeeding, however, is a complex skill to learn, and it is best taught by an experienced and successful handfeeder. It also requires a total commitment on your part, since the babies have to be fed every few hours *around the clock*. And although the process of administering food to the baby is not at all difficult, a handfed chick can get

At three months, young conures are ready to explore the world; you can bring them outdoors only with extreme caution.

The rewards of breeding are great, as demonstrated by this healthy example of a Sun conure.

sick and die very fast from complications in the feeding. Knowing what to watch out for and what to do in the event of a problem are things you need expert training in. Do not be fooled by how easily baby birds feed from a syringe.

In order to avoid any contribution, however unintended, to the improper handfeeding of baby conures, I will give no instructions in this book, and I advise that this is not something you can do after reading a little bit about it or seeing someone do it once or twice. If you want to learn, get proper training and education first; otherwise, leave the handfeeding to experts.

CO-PARENTED

A small but determined group of breeders practice co-parenting, where they leave the babies with their parents but also remove them at times and play with and hand-feed them. This can be very successful, producing babies that are naturally raised but still imprinted on humans. It requires, however, very cooperative parent birds. Even the sweetest hand-tame parrots can become vicious and suspicious when nesting, and all too often their response to this kind of intervention can be to abandon or even destroy the chicks. Sometimes the male will kill the female in frustration, as if she were to blame for the humans taking the chicks out of the box. If you want to try co-parenting, make sure that your birds trust you completely, and that you keep a close eye on their reactions. Similar results can be more safely achieved by leaving the babies with the parents for a month and then pulling them for handfeeding, though this is more risky for the babies themselves and much more time-consuming for the breeder.

The Birds

PETITE PYRRHURAS

If conures are macaws in miniature, then pyrrhuras are mini conures. At first glance you might group them with the grass parakeets, but what they lack in size, they make up for in personality. These little clowns make affectionate and fearless companions, and some of them even learn to talk. When handfed and raised, they pack big parrot behavior into a tiny package.

This group has a great many species with a great many subspecies, and there is often only a subtle variation between them. The major difference between the two most available species, the Maroon-Bellied and the Green-Cheeked, is the greenish patch on the cheeks of the latter. This explains the otherwise odd name of the Green-Cheeked conure. When I saw my first specimen, I laughed, say-ing the only thing that wasn't green on them was their cheeks. A second look proved that their cheeks are, indeed,

The Green-Cheeked conure is one of the more available *Pyrrhura* conures.

The Maroon-Bellied conure is a smallish bird suited to apartment-style living.

tinged with green, but the overall impression they give is of a largely green bird with a gray head. Their delicate beauty is enhanced by a scalloped effect, with feathers edged in black.

These conures often use a nest box all year, usually preferring to sleep in one even when not nesting. As hand-raised pets they are a delight, and they seem like large parrots in tiny bodies. Their voices are proportionately small as well and less likely to pierce the ear than those of their larger cousins; they are often touted as "apartment conures."

HERE COME THE SUNS

Whenever you find separate popula-

tions of obviously closely related organisms, with little or no overlap in their ranges, they may be "races," or subspecies of one species. If, however, the geographical isolation continues long enough (in geological time), then separate species will be the result. Making that decision is not always easy, although it is easier today with the advancements in DNA sequencing. Such is the case with the *Aratinga* conures.

The most recent taxonomic revisions have removed most of the species once placed in the genus *Aratinga* and erected the genera *Thectocercus*, *Eupsittula*, *Psittacara*, and *Guaruba* for them. The conures left in *Aratinga* include the older species *A. auricapilla*, *A. solstitialis*, *A. aurifrons*, and *A. jan-*

The Gold-Capped (or Gold-Headed) conure is a native of South America.

The typical conure colors of yellow, green and red are most intermixed in the Sun conure, a largely yellow bird with green splashes and red highlights.

daya—the Golden-Capped (Headed) conure, Sun conure, Gold-Fronted conure, and Jenday conure. These are now recognized as subspecies of one species, either *A. auricapilla* or *A. solstitialis*, depending on which authority you follow.

Their natural distribution roughly follows the large eastern hump of South America, with the Sun the northernmost, followed by the Jenday, Gold-Capped, then Gold-Fronted. These birds are all similarly colored; in fact, young Jendays and young Suns can be difficult to tell apart. The plethora of hybrids out there only complicates the matter.

It is easier to illustrate the differences among these populations than to describe them. They all share the colors green, blue, reddish orange, and yellow; it's how the colors are distributed that differs. In the Sun, they are the most intermixed, with green splashed over a largely yellow body with red highlights. In the Jenday, the yellow coalesces into a solid yellow head, leaving the body and wings green; the red is also brought together on the abdomen. In the Golden-Capped, the green predominates, with the yellow confined to the head, and the red retreating into the sides of the belly. With the Gold-Fronted, the yellow is even further restricted, to the forehead, and the bird is basically green.

Although Sun conures immediately attract attention with their vibrant colors, they hold interest with their lively behavior. Born acrobats, they love to hang upside down, perform flips, and clown around. A favorite trick is to "play dead," lying on their back in your outstretched hand. They are also vociferous, chattering all the while, and sometimes screeching. A single pet bird can usually be persuaded to turn its vocal talents more to imitation than to irritation, but this is not a species for the apartment dweller.

The Jenday conure is one of the Aratingas and the one most often confused with the Sun conure.

LONG LIVE THE QUEEN!

The Queen of Bavaria conure, *Guaruba guarouba*, makes a spectacular pet—beautiful and intelligent. However, there is a case against keep-

Sun conures are lively and will attract attention with their vibrant colors and clownish behavior.

ing these birds as pets. Their fragile status means that captive breeding programs must take precedence; our sacrifice today can make it possible for future generations to be able to enjoy these beautiful birds. Even hand-raised individuals should be kept in breeding programs. Outside the breeding season they can be enjoyed as companions, but it is important to ensure the existence of this species, at least in captivity.

THE NANDAY

Related to the Sun conure and just as full of personality is the less flamboy-ant Nanday, the monotypic *Nandayus nanday*. The same types of adjectives describe this popular pet—fun-loving,

The Nanday's somber coloration often overshadows the bird's reputation as a great pet.

The Queen of Bavaria conure is kept in limited numbers because of its fragile status.

Though not as common as the Sun and Nanday, the Peach-Fronted conure makes a sweet companion.

comical, acrobatic...and noisy.

Although a Nanday caged next to a Sun in a pet shop might be overlooked because of its less flamboyant color scheme—overall green with a black head, the Nanday makes as wonderful a pet as the Sun conure. And, it is only in such a context that the beauty of the Nanday might go unnoticed. With its black head, green body, bright blue flights, and red "socks" on its legs, the Nanday is a beautiful bird in its own right. To my mind it appears a bit like a smaller version of the Patagonian.

If you ask a Nanday owner about the noise their birds make, you will generally get the reply that they are extremely noisy, but well worth putting up with. The birds simply exude personality and charm, and like doting parents anywhere, Nanday owners tend to completely overlook their faults.

GOOD LITTLE PARROTS

"Good little parrot" is the meaning behind the genus name *Eupsittula*, and the conures in this group are certainly wonderful little parrots. Although, as I indicated before, these birds are a taxonomic mess at the moment, biologists' confusion doesn't hinder our enjoyment of these conures as pets. The Peach-Fronted conure, *E. aurea*, and the Dusky-Headed, *E. weddellii*, seem to be the most available currently, though none of them is as common as Suns, Nandays, and Blue-Fronts.

Once classified as *Aratinga*, these generally smaller conures appear to be intermediate between the larger conures and the tiny *Pyrrhura* species. They also seem somewhat like the *Brotogeris* parrots. Some are talkers, but for the most part they are simply sweet pets when hand-raised. They can, as any conures can, be loud, but they don't have the power behind their voices that the larger species do. The Dusky-Headed in particular is known for being a quiet conure and is often suggested for people concerned about the effect of loud screeching on neighbors or family members.

The Dusky-Headed conure is noted for being one of the quieter conures.

RED HEADS

The genus *Psittacara* is fairly well represented in the hobby, but it is certain that there are many hybrids around. I have heard otherwise knowledgeable breeders claim that this or that *Psittacara* species is "the same as" another. The birds are known by various common names, usually but not always associated in this way: *Psittacara chloroptera*, Hispaniolan conure; *P. erythrogenys*, Red-Masked conure; *P. euops*, Cuban conure; *P. holochlora*, Green conure; *P. leucophthalmus*, White-Eyed conure; *P. mitrata*, Mitred conure; and *P. wagleri*, Wagler's conure. Other obvious names like Cherry-Headed or Red-Fronted conure are also found.

What complicates identification is that often the birds do not develop

The Wagler's conure has less red on its forehead then the Red-Masked conure.

their full red coloration for several years, and there are vast differences in the amount and placement of the red coloration even between individuals of the same species. Many juveniles are completely green, or green with a few red feathers on the head.

Once again, however, taxonomic confusion does not detract from these birds as companions. Many of the conures in this group live as special pets. They can be very macaw-like in their demand for attention and personal interaction with their owners, but they repay this attention with undying love and trust. Many individuals turn their extremely ample vocal talents to mimicry and become rather good talkers.

QUAKERS & MONKS

Called by these two religious names, *Myiopsitta monachus* is a parrot that raises very strong emotions in peo-

ple—including state legislators, since it is illegal to possess this species in several states. The reason for the governmental concern is that this bird, native to the temperate regions of South America, is quite capable of surviving in northern climates. In large numbers the birds could theoretically be quite destructive of farmers' crops, hence the concern.

The threat is more imagined than real, however. Quakers are not nomadic or migratory; they live out their entire lives within a short distance of where they were hatched. There are already breeding populations in several states, including Florida, New York, and Connecticut. The major source of the northeastern population was an accident at New York's John F. Kennedy International Airport, where some crates of Quakers from Argentina broke open, releasing the birds. These were wild-caught animals, used to caring for themselves. In some areas there have been wild colonies for many years, and they have not grown to become agricultural pests.

In fact, Quaker parrots are probably the most controllable species, due to their nesting habits. For the most part, parrots do not build nests, instead using holes and cavities of various types as nesting sites. A notable exception are the lovebirds of the genus *Agapornis*, which build nests within a nest hole. Quakers,

The Red-Masked conure is one of the Psittacara species, denoted by tell-tale red markings.

The green conure is sometimes noted for its demanding but devoted nature.

however, represent an interesting diversion in parrot evolution in this regard. Not only are they nest builders, meaning that they do not nest in natural cavities but instead build independent structures and create their own nest holes, but they do this communally. Working together, a flock will amass a large pile of sticks, twigs, and other material at the top of a tree or utility pole. Each pair then adds their own "apartment" to the structure, with chambers in which they raise their young. It is very easy to locate a Quaker nest, or to destroy it. Since it is not necessary to hunt down individual nest holes, a Quaker population can easily be controlled in the event that feral birds become a problem. Nevertheless, some legislators see fit to ban this one species of parrot, despite the fact that there is no evidence it is any more a threat than any other bird.

On the other hand, Quaker owners sing their pets' praises loudly, and with good reason. Quakers are intelligent, friendly, and garrulous birds, and they make excellent pets. Their major drawback is that even compared to noisy conures like Suns, they are loud, raucous birds. The flip side of this, however, is that they are naturally talkative and are considered among the best talkers outside of African Greys and Amazon parrots.

Their mischievous, fun-loving personalities quickly endear them to their human "flock," and they are among the most popular pet parrots. Many of them are never caged, spending all of their time with their human family—

eating, showering, or just sitting around watching television with them.

Quakers are prolific and are often available more inexpensively than any other conure. If you are interested in this species, check your local regulations, and if the birds are not restricted where you live, you can enjoy one as a delightful and charming companion bird.

BLUE-CROWNS

This species became an instant favorite of mine when I acquired my first breeding pair. They have a subtle beauty, a definite intelligence, and a quiet, sedate (for a conure) personality. At first they may appear to be a solid green bird, but a turn of the head, or a change in viewing angle for you, and their blue heads become apparent. More an iridescent sheen than a blatant pigmentation, the blue head is blended into the overall green coloration, and it is intensified in sunlight. Each time the bird moves, the color shifts from green to green-blue to blue. And this is not the only now-you-see-it-now-you-don't coloration for this species; there is a delicate copper-gold overwash to their wings and backs that is equally dependent on the exact angle at which light hits the feathers.

Known also as the Sharp-Tailed conure, they have a prominent and decidedly tapered tail, maroon underneath. They are large—about 15 inches long. Their heads are large, as is their beak, and their white eye-ring is distinct, all of which make them look like a tiny macaw. The resemblance carries over into their behavior. While their Sun or Nanday cousins are busy turning somersaults and swinging upside-down, the Blue-Crowns will be standing on a perch, carefully surveying the area, or calmly climbing beak over feet across the top of their cage. Like macaws, these birds enjoy playing, and they can be quite lively; compared to the smaller conures, however, they are more staid.

The Mitred conure is a species in which the amount of red coloration may vary between individuals.

Cherry-Headed and Red-Fronted are common names often interchanged with members of the *Psittacara* genus.

Also like macaws, they do not have the clamorous personalities of the Suns and Jendays, but when they do choose to vocalize, it is proportionately louder! While I might call the smaller conures' vocalizations "chattering," the Blue- Crowns' seem more purposeful—a squawk here, a whistle there, reserving the big blasts of noise for a directed communication.

PATAGONIANS

This large conure is not too common in aviculture, but it occurs in very large flocks in its native southern South America, where it nests in burrows in rocky cliffs. In one of those vicious paradoxes of life, here is a bird that would be welcomed by many breeders and pet owners but that is exterminated in large numbers by farmers in its natural range, who are plagued with huge flocks of the birds descending on their crops and ravaging them. In some places, the chicks are consumed by humans as a delicacy.

When available and hand-raised, a Patagonian makes a fine pet, but it is also important to see these birds in breeding programs so that they can be firmly established in captive strains. Experience teaches the unfortunate lesson that an agricultural pest today can quickly become an extinct species tomorrow.

ONWARD

In this book we have been unable to do much more than scratch the surface in our review of the various species of conures. You may find a conure for sale that has not been covered, and there is much more to say about the ones we have.

With an understanding of the basics of conure care in the first part of the book, you should be able to keep any species happy and healthy. It is my hope that this second section has given you enough information to narrow down your choices. You can then go on to research those conures that most interest you in more detail. Whatever your choice, I am sure you will have many years of enjoyment and friendship with your conure, since all of these beautiful, intelligent animals make wonderful pets.

Enjoy your conure!

Resources

AFA Watchbird

American Federation of Aviculture, Inc.
P.O. Box 56218
Phoenix, AZ 85079
www.afa.birds.org

The AFA is a nonprofit organization dedicated to the promotion of aviculture and the conservation of avian wildlife through the encouragement of captive-breeding programs, scientific research, and the education of the general public. The AFA publishes a bi-monthly magazine called AFA Watchbird.

Association of Avian Veterinarians

P.O. Box 811720
Boca Raton, FL 33481
561-393-8901
www.aav.org

AAV membership is comprised of veterinarians from private practice, zoos, universities and industry, veterinary educators, researchers and technicians, and veterinary students. Serves as resource for bird owners who are looking for certified avian veterinarians.

Bird Times

Pet Publishing, Inc.
7-L Dundas Circle
Greensboro, NC 27407
www.birdtimes.com

Bird Times is a source of entertaining and authoritative information about birds. Articles include bird breed profiles, medical reports, training advice, bird puzzles, and stories about special birds.

The Gabriel Foundation

P.O. Box 11477
Aspen, CO 81612
www.thegabrielfoundation.org

The Gabriel Foundation is a nonprofit organization dedicated to promoting education, rescue, adoption, and sanctuary for parrots.

Midwest Avian Research Expo (MARE)

10430 Dewhurst Rd.
Elyria, OH 44036
www.mare-expo.org

MARE is a nonprofit group dedicated to education and fundraising for avian research projects.

National Animal Poison Control Center/ASPCA

888-426-4435
900-680-0000

In a life-and-death poisoning situation you can call this hotline for 24-hour emergency information. Please note that there is a charge for this service.

Index

Photo Credits

Photographs by: Joan Balzarini, Delia Berlin, Isabelle Francais, H. Mayer, Robert Pearcy, and John Tyson.